My Saturdad Boys Weekend

Written by
Neil David Ewan and Kristian William Wright
Illustrated by
Neil David Ewan

All intellectual/copywrites belong to Neil David Ewan and Kristian William Wright
Published by Kristian William Wright

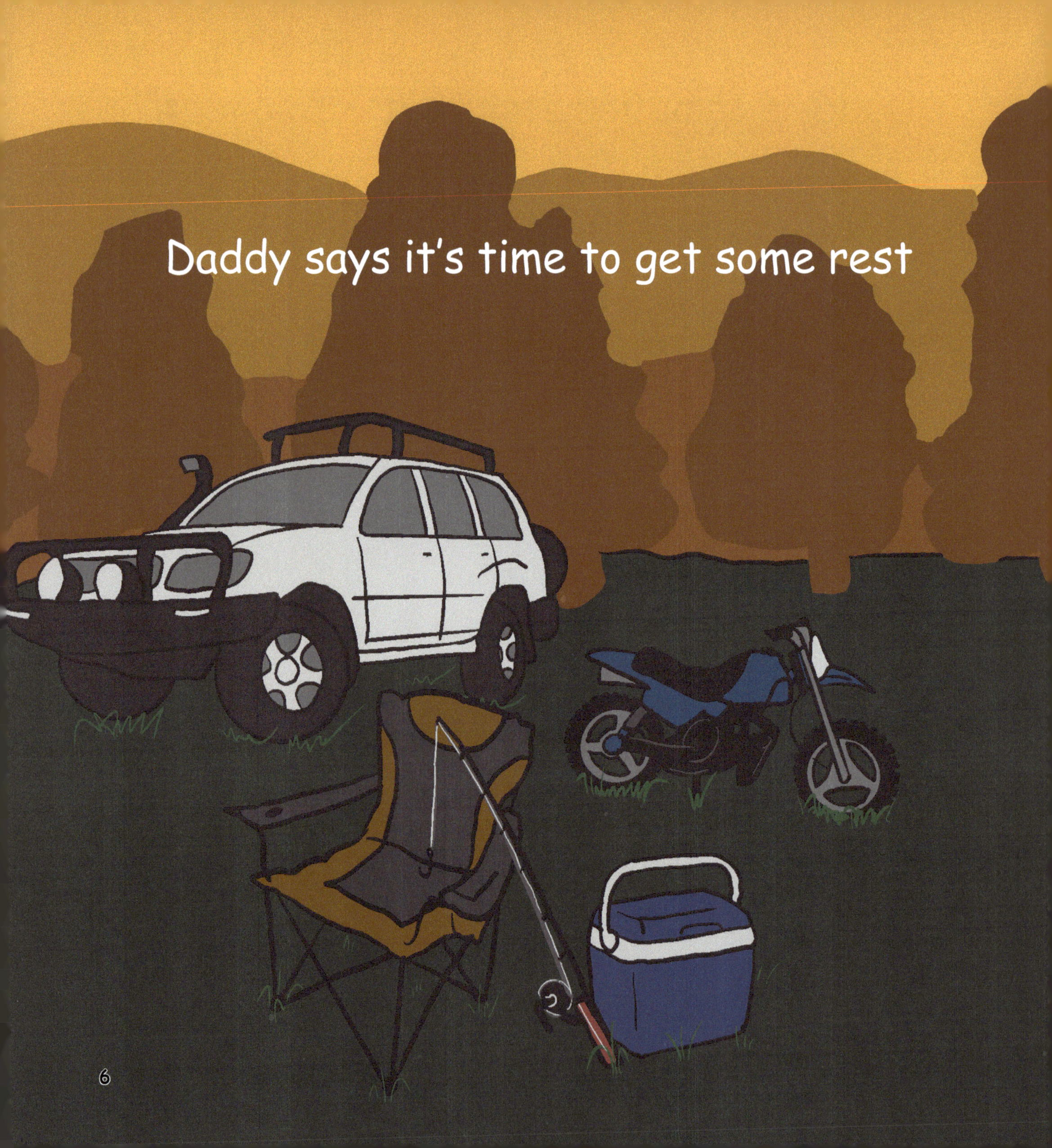

Daddy says it's time to get some rest

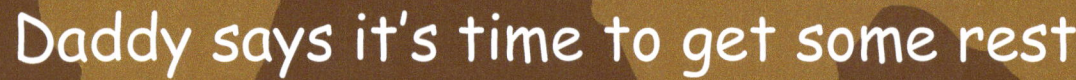

I wake up in the morning,
we rise before the sun

My daddy and I have breakfast,
now we're ready for fun

I know my Saturdad loves me,
with every piece of his heart

I know that never changes,
even when we are apart

My Dad Loves Me!

(Write a letter to your child to let them know how much you love them)

Colour Me In!

*'He who has a why to live can
bear almost any how.'*
- Friedrich Nietzsche

No matter how hard it gets, no matter how much it hurts
and no matter how many obstacles they put in your way,
never give up on your children. They need you.

www.mysaturdad.com

www.ingramcontent.com/pod-product-compliance
Lightning Source LLC
Chambersburg PA
CBHW041526070526
44585CB00002B/107